Beekeeping 101:
Why I keep honey bees
(and why you should, too!)

Keys to Your Success

Grant F. C. Gillard

Beekeeping 101:
Why I keep honey bees
(and why you should, too!)

Keys to Your Success

Copyright 2012 by Grant F. C. Gillard

For more information:

Grant F.C. Gillard
3721 North High Street
Jackson, MO 63755
gillard5@charter.net

Grant F.C. Gillard has been keeping bees since 1981. He speaks at bee conferences and conventions across the nation. Contact him at gillard5@charter.net to check his availability.

Dedication:

This is my first "real" book in print.

I want to dedicate this book to my loving wife of twenty-six years, the mother of our three children who are now grown and have flown the nest, thanks in large part to her capable and strengthening nurture.

Nancy has been a devoted cheerleader of my writing and has patiently persisted with my passionate, often obsessive fascination with the honeybees, an activity to which she lovingly describes as my "hobby on steroids."

Few beekeepers are as fortunate as me.

Acknowledgement:

This book would not be possible without the guidance from my writing coach, Linda Culbreth.

I marvel at God's providence for opening the door to her Wednesday Night Writing Class. Linda is a gracious encourager and practices what she preaches, a shining testament of a willing servant.

Thanks to Linda's class, I am a published author. Without her persistent accountability, I would merely be a writer.

Beekeeping 101:
Why I keep honey bees (and why you should, too!)

Keys to Your Success

Table of Contents

Introduction:

Have you ever wanted to keep honeybees and become a bee keeper? Maybe you saw an ad in the newspaper for "bees for sale," or you saw some beekeepers at the local farmers market selling organic honey. Perhaps you read about local raw honey and wanted the benefit of honey for health. Perhaps you wanted to study apiculture and establish an apiary (so you can be called an apiarist!). Or you've always wanted to get into the bee removal business for nervous homeowners demanding that you, "get rid of bees."

Since 1981, I've been a beekeeper. I sell bee products. I tell bee facts. I've done bee hive removal. I've endured thousands of stings and owned several honey extractors. One of my growing markets is for natural honey and comb honey. People buy my honey for allergies. I make my own bee hives and sell beekeeper supplies as well as teach beekeeping courses.

Every day (or so it seems) someone asks me how I got into beekeeping, how I decided to raise bees as well as produce my own queen honeybees. They ask me if I produce royal jelly. They want to know how many times I've been stung. The conversation soon drifts to a timid request wondering if I would help them start raising honey bees. Would I mentor them? Do I have any used beekeeping equipment for sale? How much does it cost to get started? Where can they buy bees? Do I have bees for sale?

In this book I probe those kinds of questions. I share my experience (the good, the bad and the wonderful!) and hopefully give anyone who is thinking about keeping bees a little "heads up." I want to share how I got into this marvelous hobby called beekeeping, but also take the perspective of what I might have done differently. Hopefully, my experience will help you decide if beekeeping is for you, and if so, how you can make the most intelligent decisions on getting started.

I wrote this book from hundreds of inquiries, phone calls and e-mails from people interested in keeping honeybees. Everyone's situation is different, everyone's budget varies, and everyone's level of commitment depends on a million different factors. There is no easy, single, one-size-fits-all answer...except my belief that, "Yes! You can keep bees."

Let's start with that premise, because I believe, with enough faith and effort, you can become a beekeeper.

Why I Keep Honey Bees:

So let me cut to the chase: why do I keep honey bees? I think of the potential dangers of keeping thousands of stinging insects in my back yard. Who in their right mind does this? Then I wonder, "Wouldn't it be safer to breed rattlesnakes or mix potentially explosive, toxic chemicals?" But isn't it just as crazy to keep honey bees within a stone's throw of my back door? Are bee keepers insane, or what?

The first reaction I get from people who know I keep bees is the threat of getting stung. Yes, I get stung. How many times? I've lost count. Seriously, I can't count how many times I get stung in just one day. I get stung so often I don't even bother to count. People ask me if I'm allergic to stings, and I casually them them the only reaction I have is mild profanity!

Getting stung is just part of the business, but I can protect myself by smoking the hive with smoke (which calms the bees). I can dress in the protective clothing that looks like a space suit (and is really hot during the middle of the summer). I can choose to open my hives on the nicest, sunniest days (when the bees are happiest because they are working!). And by doing these things, I can greatly reduce the chances of getting stung.

There are ways to get around the threat of getting stung. And seriously, yes, there are some days I don't get stung, but I don't always have nice days to work my hives. Some days it's too hot for that full-bodied bee suit. As for me, I just accept getting stung as part of the business of keeping honeybees. You may find getting stung is a bigger issue and it will quickly dim any enthusiasm you have for keeping bees.

So why do I keep bees? I keep bees because I enjoy it. I enjoy managing a hive of bees and watching them respond to my management. I like helping the bees get the most productivity out of their potential. I like collaborating with the Created Order, assisting Nature to produce its best. I like harvesting honey as my reward. I like meeting people at the farmers markets and selling honey. I like what I'm able to do with the money I make selling honey. I like everything about keeping honey bees, and I don't mind the stings.

I also like working outdoors. And despite the poison ivy, the chiggers, ticks and snakes, I like being outdoors. My wife, on the other hand, is a self-described "indoorsy kind of girl." I like camping. She prefers a motel with room service. I don't mind the heat and humidity. She doesn't care for anything that makes her break a sweat. And don't get me wrong. I love this woman to death. She just prefers a different kind of work in a different environment, but she supports me in my endeavors to keep bees (and she's also grown fond of the financial rewards of selling that honey I produce!).

But most of all, I enjoy keeping honey bees. I've often wondered if I ever won the lottery, and I could do whatever I wanted to do, even if it wasn't work-related, what would I do? Being an instant millionaire, I could whatever I wanted to do. So what would I do? I think if I became an instant, lottery millionaire, I would still keep bees. I would still set up at the farmers markets and sell honey. I would still battle the heat and the humidity. I would still fight the snakes, chiggers and ticks. I would still plough through the poison ivy. I keep bees for the fun of it. I keep bees because I enjoy doing it. To some people beekeeping sounds like a lot of work, but is it really work if you enjoy it?

And there's an old expression:

"The person who enjoys what they do
never works a day in their life."

The wife of one of my beekeeping buddies was getting a little snippy one day. I said I was planning to order some nucleus colonies from Florida to both sell to others and to expand my bee yards. She snipped, "Well, that just sounds like a lot of work to me."

I simply replied, in a very nice and courteous manner, "Well, it sounds like work, but it smells like money."

And she was right. It's work. But I enjoy the activities so much I don't mind the work. Maybe I'm a glutton for punishment, but I enjoy keeping bees. I just like keeping bees. I also like the rewards that beekeeping offers. Some of them are financial, but many of the rewards are social. I'm known locally as the "honey dude" or the "bee man" in my community. I do quite a business of removing swarms. But that's a topic for a later date.

The bottom line for me is I keep bees because I enjoy it. If it's not something you enjoy and if you don't enjoy working outside in the heat, then beekeeping is probably not for you. If you can't tolerate the bee stings, then maybe collecting stamps is more your cup of tea where the worst that can happen is receiving a paper cut.

The first reason I keep honey bees is because I like doing it. I enjoy working with these industrious little insects.

A second reason I keep bees is that it provides me with a distraction from my "real" job. My real job, one that puts groceries on the table, gives me medical benefits and socks away money for my retirement is that of Presbyterian Pastor. Being pastor is a 24/7 job that deals with a lot of personal issues as well as running the administration of a church and providing spiritual counsel. And don't get me wrong. I love my work as pastor!

I apply the same lottery millionaire question to preaching and pastoring. If I won the lottery, would I keep working at the church? And as I've pondered this question, I come up with a definite, "Yes!" I would still do weddings and funerals and visit the nursing home. I would still preach and pastor. And though I can retire early at the age of 55, I still like what I do and so I'm not looking toward retiring anytime soon.

But sometimes I need a daily sabbatical. Sometimes I need to get away from the office, shut off my cell phone, walk out into the woods and tend to my bees. They provide me with a necessary respite. Everyone needs some form of recreation. Some of my pastor friends play golf. Some are artists. Some of them restore old cars. The bottom line is everyone needs something to fill them up from a job that often empties them of their creativity and imagination. Beekeeping does that for me.

The third reason I keep bees because they help me see the Divine in the Created Order. I walk into the woods and watch those bees work so diligently. I open the hives and I see the architecture of the hive taught by the Great Architect. I watch the queen do her business and the social order that maintains the productivity of the hive. How can I not see God at work? The inner workings of the hive are amazing. The hive works like a large clock with all of its ratchets and sprockets, all timed perfectly. Beekeeping lets me be part of this Divine Order and participate in its management.

And then there is the money. I produce honey to sell for money. People see me at the farmers markets with a table full of product and a cash box full of money. They look longingly and ask, "Gee, Grant. Can a person make a living from keeping bees?"

The answer is, "Yes," but it depends on how astutely you manage your colonies and how intelligently you market your honey. But there are some risks and for the sake of my family, I'm not quite ready to abandon my medical insurance and pension to take on beekeeping as a full-time endeavor. I still have kids in college. I'm not ready to quit my day job.

But then are some days in which I think maybe I will. There are some days I want to. But I do enjoy being a pastor and it likewise gives me a break from beekeeping.

Could I make a living keeping bees and selling honey? The easy answer is, "Yes! It's possible to make a living keeping honeybees." But it depends on many factors, and like any agricultural venture, you are subject to weather and other variables. Like anything in farming, it's a lot of work that doesn't fit the 9-5 routines of Monday through Friday. I still keep bees on a part-time basis and yet I fully enjoy the extra income it brings in to supplement my salary as a preacher. I'm not ready to quit my day job.

Would I Do Things Differently?:

Sometimes we ponder the possibility that if we had it all to do over again, would we? What would we change? What would we do differently? And it's something I think about every day for all areas of my life. They say hindsight is 20/20, meaning you can view the past perfectly and with absolute clarity. We see our mistakes so clearly. We know there are things we would avoid.

So I take the perspective, that if I had to start beekeeping all over again, what would I change? What mistakes did I make that I would avoid? What advice would I give the person who approaches me at the farmers market and asks, "Can you help me get started in bees?" Are there things that I did that I would counsel against?

In the hindsight of 20/20 clarity, of course, there are things I would definitely change. But there a host of lessons I learned along the way that cannot be simplified into three-step programs for success or a five-minute conversation over my table at the farmers market.

When people come to me and ask me if I'll get them started keeping bees, the first thing I say is, "Sure, I can get you started." But different people need different kinds of help. Some just need to be pointed in the right direction with the permission to, "You go, girl!" (Yes, there are many women getting into beekeeping.)

Others who ask for my assistance seem to require a great deal of hand-holding. They seem to need me to show them by doing. I used to bring people out to my yards and together we would open hives and I'd show them what I do. Years ago, I had time to go out and work a hive for a new beekeeper. Today, there's just not enough time in the day to do this kind of teaching. But I'll still help someone get started. I just can't put as much time into the mentoring as I used to.

It seems many people will catch the idea of keeping bees in the late spring and early summer when everything around us is blooming. The ideal time to get started is in the winter when you can order your supplies, assemble and paint them, and put in an order for either a package of bees or a nucleus colony (nicknamed, "nucs").

So if you are getting interested in keeping bees, I would suggest you first find your local beekeeper and ask if there is a local club or meeting you can attend. Go to these meetings and listen to what others are doing. Beekeeping varies from region to region and beekeepers in your area will have their own seasonality to what they do.

At the meeting, ask about beginner classes. Today, beekeeping is catching a lot of attention and more and more clubs are forming. These clubs offer beginner classes, usually in February, but you'll need to sign up for them earlier. These classes often fill up to capacity.

These same clubs will also guide you in what equipment to order, and if it's a club worth its salt, they will place a large order on behalf of the club to pool all the individual orders and save money on bulk discounts and shipping charges. The club should also arrange orders for beginners to acquire bees.

Now all of this is done in February. Most people don't catch the idea of beekeeping until late spring or early summer and it's really too late to get the equipment ordered. By the time these people do get their equipment assembled and painted, there are no bees available. There's a seasonality to beekeeping that will greatly affect your success. But most people interested in beekeeping don't realize the time to get ready is before the weather is suitable to get started.

Now I didn't have any bee clubs in my area when I started keeping honey bees. You can successfully get started without a local bee club. I didn't have a mentor. I didn't have Internet access to join an on-line forum for advice. I just did it. You too, if you are attuned to the myriad of details, can effectively establish a colony of honeybees in the middle of the summer, even early fall. But it's more difficult, and harder, still, if you don't know what you are doing or if you've just jumped into keeping bees and you're unfamiliar with the seasonality. So my rather stern, fatherly advice is not to rush into this endeavor.

Get to know some beekeepers through a bee club. Ask, if they have time, to go with them and open up some hives (most small beekeepers have time and welcome the opportunity to show you their bees). Sign up for beginner classes in the winter. Ask what equipment you're going to need. Make sure and order your equipment early and secure your order of honeybees well before warm weather arrives.

If it's summer and you're just now getting interested, it's likely a little too late. Build the launching platform now for next spring's blast-off! Early spring is the best time to get started, however, with enough mentor support, bees can be started at other times during the growing season...but it's trickier.

Fair Warning:

I find there is a high degree of romance associated with beekeeping. The average person has no idea what they are getting into. They only see beekeeping as a noble endeavor producing a natural product.

I want to share a little reality check. Bee keeping is, indeed, a noble venture and the industriousness of the honey bee elevates the work of the beekeeper to near sainthood. With the potential to receive painful episodes of stings, the work of the bee keeper reaches the dedication of a martyr (or maybe a glutton for punishment).

The advice I hope to share are my thoughts about beekeeping from people who have asked me to help them get started. One of my leading thoughts is how I would set up my hives if I had the opportunity to do it all over again. Knowing what I know now, how would that knowledge shape my decisions or change my strategy back in the beginning? I hope to impart those lessons of what worked, what's the best way to get started, and how can I lower the elevation of your learning curve.

The first warning is that beekeeping is an expensive hobby to initiate. It's not too bad once you become established. In a later chapter I'll share some of the expenses that must be paid up front.

The second warning is that bees die. You can pay for a hive of bees only to have them die the next winter. Or they will totally abscond and leave the hive. Or they'll succumb to a disease. And all your money invested in the bees will die along with them.

My third warning is that this hobby is also very enjoyable and extremely addictive. One gentleman came to our local bee club and said he wanted to start keeping bees, saying, "My wife said I could keep two hives in the yard and that's all I want to do." We offered him advice, got him started and he took off like a rocket.

Two hives. Yeah, famous last words. He's in his fourth year now and he manages thirty hives. Now bear in mind, these thirty hives are not all in his back yard. He found some people who wanted hives on their farm and his hobby was able to expand. We'll talk more about expansion issues and where to best keep bees. But heed my warning: beekeeping is fun and can result in keeping more and more hives. Inform your spouse of this danger. They'll think you've lost your mind when you tell them you want to add more hives next year!

As beekeeping takes a substantial financial investment, it pains my heart to see first- and second-year beekeepers lose heart and quit. Then they have the sorry task of selling their used equipment in a vain attempt to capture their initial costs.

Along with this task of selling their used equipment comes the confession that they couldn't do it. They could not master this art of beekeeping. Time, energy and money have been invested and they come up deflated and discouraged. But beekeeping is not for everyone. It takes special skills unrelated to beekeeping to stay in business. Then there are those hearty souls who are eager to keep bees but they find they are allergic to the bee venom they receive when they are stung. It's very sad.

When people stop me and we visit about starting a couple of hives in the back yard, I try to paint a reasonable picture. They have many questions and my answers come with the conditional disclaimer: "Well, all things being equal…" (and they never are). Beekeeping is a whole lot more involved than putting a hive in the back yard and harvesting gallons of honey. It just doesn't work that way.

I must confess the questions from prospective beekeepers are overwhelming because there are no easy answers, and as much as I try to keep my answers easy to understand, my answers are anything but simple. I give answers based on my experience, and yet the lack of familiarity from those who ask the questions prevents a clear understanding of what it takes to keep bees.

It's like gardening. There is more to gardening than planting a seed, waiting the 62 days to maturity, then harvesting ten bushels of ripe produce. There are so many variables with weather, rainfall, temperatures, frost, bugs and diseases that one cannot reduce gardening to a formula of plant-this-then-harvest-that. And the produce you pull off the vine looks NOTHING like the picture on the seed packet.

Additionally, beekeepers tend to talk a foreign language of jargon, slang and idioms. We have our own lingo. Our speech is littered with lots of abbreviated acronyms that sound like an alphabet soup. Trying to explain bee keeping is much more than a five-minute conversation in the aisle at the grocery store.

And when I'm approached to help get someone started or mentor them, they have no concept of how much time this hobby entails, and how little time I have to spare getting them started and how much they have to discover on their own. I have my own hives to take care of as well as family obligations and work commitments. I can't do everything for these new beekeepers. And yet the journey of keeping bees is mired with many trials and snares.

No Easy Answers:

There are no easy, simple, logical answers to keeping bees. Beekeeping is "more art than science," and you cannot always depend upon predictable and reliable results.

Bee keeping is "local," that is, each area in which bee keepers keep honey bees has its own set of localized, idiosyncratic, unique and complex set of circumstances. What works in Montana won't fly in Minnesota and is doomed for failure in Mississippi.

The skills required for beekeeping are more often "caught" than "taught." I often recommend reading books on beekeeping, but head knowledge does not translate into hand skill. It's like reading books about how to swim. Knowledge is great, but until you jump into the water, you don't know what it takes to swim.

There are times I wonder if beekeepers are born rather than made. And even after all these years of keeping bees, I'm still learning.

The education never stops and the bees continue to teach this old dog a number of new tricks.

The learning curve isn't really high, it's just steep. Then it plateaus to a long, rising grade of continual learning. It's been said that the bees make better beekeepers then beekeepers make bees. When the student is ready, the teacher appears. Bees are the best teachers.

But don't let me deter your interest in keeping bees. Let me begin my apiarian story by sharing how I got my start in beekeeping, and why I'm still keeping bees today.

Inauspicious Beginnings:

In 1977, I enrolled at Iowa State University in Ames, Iowa, attending the College of Agriculture. My real interest in choosing Iowa State University was their trapshooting club. Through my high school years in Albert Lea, Minnesota, I was a competitive trap shooter, winning a number of local and state honors. I was pretty good and I wanted to continue my interest in trap shooting on the college level.

In the spring of 1978, still in my freshman year shooting on the ISU Trap & Skeet Club, I broke 196 out of 200 clay pigeons (with a 25-straight in a shoot off against the previous year's defending champion) to win the national collegiate championships held in Peoria, Illinois. I was the number one, college trap shooter in the nation!

While it sounds like I arrogantly digress from the topic of beekeeping, that story is what brought me to ISU. And it was my choice of attending Iowa State University to pursue my love of trap shooting that surreptitiously defined my fate as a beekeeper.

Like many new college students, I wandered as I wondered with what to do with my life. My family had an agricultural background as both my parents grew up on small, diversified farms in rural Minnesota during the Great Depression. They were snug with their money and never threw anything away that couldn't be repaired or reused. They remembered tough times and cherished the value of hard work. They knew application yielded advancement and those lessons were not wasted on me. I consider my frugality a genetically-inflicted impairment that served me well as I began my beekeeping hobby after graduation.

Like many college freshmen, I spent that first year learning…learning how to go to college, learning how to study and learning how to meet the unexplained expectations of the professors. It was a challenging time. What had served me so well in high school wasn't working in college.

When I sat down with my advisor in my sophomore year to select my classes for the next quarter, it was obvious I needed some easy electives to boost my grade point average. I had already used up some music credits and physical education credits, and had done quite well, but I needed something just as easy. I needed a slam-dunk, no-brainer course that would deliver the guaranteed "A."

As my advisor listed off the courses, he mentioned an art class (nick-named, "underwater basket weaving"), a geology course (nick-named, "rocks for jocks" because all the football players frequented this class), and dismissively mentioned Entomology 222, "Beekeeping," with the sarcastic statement, "but that's for the granola crowd, you know, the nuts and flakes."

Having grown up in an agriculturally-minded family, the lessons my mother taught me of pollination and the benefits of honey bees was a perennial tutorial. She was an avid gardener and something was always blooming in our yard. I grew up with an arm-chair awareness of honey bees and their vital role in agriculture.

While I didn't consider myself part of the "granola crowd," the idea of taking a class studying beekeeping appealed greatly to me. I had no idea what the class required. I had no grandiose plans of producing honey nor any knowledge of how honey was produced. But I wanted to enroll. I remember my advisor rolling his eye saying, "Okay. Whatever."

The class was taught by a retired, high school biology teacher named Richard Trump. On Tuesday afternoons we met in the class room and he lectured and explained the deep sociological intricacies of the honey bee colony. He explained the role of the queen honey bee and the role of the foragers as they gathered pollen and nectar. Everything worked because every bee did their work. It was amazing stuff, especially considering this was all done in the dark, inside one of those little white boxes.

On Thursday afternoons we met in the university apiary (what others might simply call the bee yard). We would break into groups of two or three students, one who would record the observations in their notebook, and the other one or two who would smoke and open the hive and point out what we talked about on the previous Tuesday. Those observations were written up and turned in to the instructor the following class period.

Mr. Trump gave two grades in this class. You either received an "A" or an "F." If you did not get stung as you smoked and opened the hives, you failed. His rationale was simple. If you didn't get stung, you were not involved in the observation of the working colony. If you didn't get stung, you received an "F." If you got stung, obviously you were working the hive and therefore, you deserved an "A." Well, I got an "A."

Actually, we all got "A's" because we all got stung.

There were no "B's" given (pun intended).

It was great fun and incredibly engrossing and intriguing. It wasn't long and I was smitten with bee keeping. That was the spring semester of 1979 and I began to make my plans to start keeping bees on the family farm upon graduation.

I subscribed to my own copies of *Gleanings in Bee Culture* and *The American Bee Journal* after discovering them in the university library. The text book for this class (which I still have) was *The Hive and the Honey Bee* (the 1975 version published by Dadant). The cover still sports the original price sticker of $9.35 from the Student Supply Store on Lincoln Way. Today, that same book sells for $50 and it's been updated and regularly revised.

Upon my graduation in 1981, I returned to the family farm in Minnesota. I took that initial step of faith and bought brand new beekeeping equipment and enough five-frame nucs for twenty bee hives. This providential day set my beekeeping career in motion.

And what I discovered was beekeeping is a lot like learning how to swim, as I've mentioned in the previous chapter. If you want to swim, you can pick up one of several books and read all about swimming. There are lots of books out there on how to swim. I recommend choosing a good book with pictures.

Armed with this knowledge, you can discuss and argue the finer points of stroke technique. You can even lift weights to make your body stronger and your stroke more effective. But until you jump into the water, you'll never learn how to swim. In fact, the best way to learn how to swim is to jump in over your head. When you find yourself in over your head, you'll either sink or swim.

The same lesson fits those of us attempting to raise honey bees. Read all the books you can find (and I highly recommend reading lots of different books from different authors, especially books with pictures). Find blogs and bulletin board services on the Internet that discuss bees and honey production and "chat" on-line with as many people on all the subjects you want. You can ask all the dumb questions that would embarrass you if asked in person. One of my college professors used to say, "There's no such thing as a dumb question." But some questions, asked by some people, sure sounded dumb to the rest of us. Asking questions is one way some people learn.

But until you get yourself a couple of hives of honey bees, you don't really know how to keep bees. And if you jump in over your head, you'll either sink or swim. Surprisingly, most of us find out how to swim!

I'm also an Eagle Boy Scout, and the toughest challenge for me to earn this rank was completing the requirements for the swimming merit badge. The lake at the summer camp where I worked on this merit badge was dark, deep and murky. Who knew what monsters lurked in wait of unsuspecting swimmers?

Our minds, and our fertile imagination, produced some of the worst fears (largely irrational) on why we could not, rather would not, jump into the lake. But we were definitely over our heads.

So it will be for most people in beekeeping. Opening a hive, fearing the stings or initiating a swarm is scary. But don't let your imagination run away. Get started, anyway!

Boldly Establishing My Apiary:

In retrospect, my initial step of faith was a bold move…perhaps even downright foolish. The experts suggest starting out with two, maybe even four hives. I got enough boxes and bees for twenty hives. It was ambitious, grandiose and gave a real-life illustration of a fool rushing in where angels fear to tread. But I wanted to keep bees. I wanted to make a living from bees. I wanted to include honeybees as part of my farming operation.

My initial vision of a farm included a multi-level, diversified, integrated series of enterprises that would take advantage of organic agricultural practices, prudent crop rotation, and would incorporate ruminant livestock which would consume roughage and provide manure for fertilizer. Honey bees would be one niche in the greater production scheme. And they would provide pollination. That was my vision.

So what did I do but take a flying leap of faith. I ordered the nucs and equipment for twenty hives. I paid cash. I made the commitment. And I was over my head from the beginning.

Where there is no vision, the people perish:

The key to successfully starting any business or enterprise is vision. Well, vision and a nice pile of cash. And luck. But definitely vision.

Without vision, people perish. Without vision, businesses flounder. Without vision people run around in circles like chickens with the heads cut off. Without vision, there is no perseverance and goals and projects soon succumb to the frustrating inconsistencies of life.

Vision begins with the end in mind. Vision asks the questions, "Where do you want to go?" Well, I had made up my mind that I would be a commercial beekeeper with the notion of selling honey for a profit. That was the end I had in mind.

But how to get from my bold beginnings to the gloriously profitable end I had in mind was plagued by my inexperience and my lack of planning. Vision can only take you so far. Boldness soon falters under the struggles and difficulties of the daily surprises that were not planned for (and could not be planned for).

And the profits I had anticipated were not easy to come by. I was fortunate to harvest honey my first year (not every new beekeeper does!). Now what? What was I going to do with my honey? How would I sell it? Who would buy it? Details, details, details! I was still running on vision and I needed a marketing plan. I also needed an inexpensive supply of pint canning jars to sell my honey.

If there is one good thing about keeping bees, it is their independence. Honeybees work without requiring a boss to tell them how to do their job and when to do it. They never go on strike and they never show up drunk. They never quit working for you in search of higher wages from someone else. They give of themselves without concern for themselves, all working for the long-term success of the colony.

I must confess there were a lot of things about raising honeybees that escaped my lack of planning, but the bees compensated for my ignorance and down-right stupidity.

Somehow, by luck or by pluck, I survived my first year. It was a tremendous learning experience and a number of times I was overwhelmed. But I was not going to concede to defeat!

Thankfully, I had a vision and it was my vision that kept me going, even if I wasn't going where I thought I would be, even though I ended up in places I never imagined. My vision would later be refined and revised. Amid the stings and oppressive heat and humidity, my vision propelled me forward.

Never underestimate your sense of vision of what you want, and if you feel you want to keep honeybees, keep that vision out in front of you. Let it plow a path for you, for each day will challenge your commitment to keeping honeybees. Let vision be your point man.

The Autonomy of the Honey Bee:

I have friends who raise free-range chickens (**http://www.familyfriendlyfarm.com**). The chickens have to be protected by guard dogs and fencing that is made into electrified netting. Feed and water must be brought to them. They take a lot of care and oversight.

Bees, on the other hand, fend for themselves and forage for their needs. No one has to insure they are working. No one has to persuade them to go to work. Honeybees work despite my incompetence and inexperience. They don't need guard dogs. They defend their own home. Bees are basically wild insects that have taught us to cater to their behavior in order that we can harvest honey.

My grandiose beginning was also back in 1981, before the varroa mite invaded the United States and parasitized our colonies. Beekeeping was easier back then. The learning curve was lower. The initial cost to get started was lower and so were honey prices.

Today starting a colony of bees is much more expensive and the price of honey only marginally higher. There are more challenges and the news stories of this mysterious disease killing our bees (called Colony Collapse Disorder or CCD) raises the learning curve to astronomical heights. It's harder today.

But on the other hand, there is more interest in beekeeping and more classes offered by experienced beekeepers. Thanks to the Internet, information and resources are more available. And the wealth of information, some of it conflicting and contradictory, can be a forest for which you cannot find the trees.

But there is one thing in our favor. The honeybees continue to show me how resilient they are to changes in weather and my incompetent, ignorant and misguided management. The honeybees humble me by surviving despite my mistakes. They are marvelously autonomous.

One of the fears of beginning beekeepers is what to do and when it needs to be done. The beauty of keeping honeybees is how they will compensate for your lack of planning. They can easily take care of themselves. Sometimes the best thing beginners can do is sit back and give the bees the chance to teach them what it means to be a beekeeper.

Your Hunger Factor:

On average, if you were to buy new equipment today, a normal hive would cost around $250 for the equipment (prices will vary depending on shipping distances and respective suppliers).

Add another $100 to $125 for the cost of bees.

This comes to around $375 for one hive and most of the experts suggest you start with a minimum of two hives, four if you can afford it. But who can afford it?

Here's the secret: Those who really want it can afford it! It's called the "hunger factor." How bad do you want it? Do you "hunger" for it? Like a lot of things in life, you got to want it to get it.

But where will the money come from? I can't count the number of people who approached me wanting to start a hive of honeybees only to be deterred because it just costs a literal arm and a leg to get started.

So how bad do you want to keep honey bees? Where will you come up with that kind of money in our current economy?

Have you ever looked at your cell phone bill? How many bells and whistles (like network access to the Internet) are you paying for each month? Have you looked at what it costs for your Internet connection on your home computer?

How many times a week do you eat out at a fast-food restaurant? How often could you have brought a lunch to work to save that money? Do you make a cup of coffee at home or do you stop for a cup of that over-priced latte described by some foreign language to differentiate the sizes?

I don't mean to scrutinize, analyze or criticize your household or personal budget, but there are places where you can find the money to start keeping bees. But you have to want it. You want other things, like cell phone service, Internet service on your cell phone, television that records to a digital format (and not to disparage your taste in technology) but if you find money for these things, I think you can find the money for bee hives.

I would use the figure of $375 for each hive, but I would also plan on a one-time cost of $100 to $150 for additional equipment like a smoker, a bee suit, etc. From there you can decide how much sacrificing it's going to take to make this beekeeping deal a reality.

I remember the guy who complained it just cost too much money to start keeping bees, but somehow he found the money for one of those fancy, flat-screen televisions the size of a sofa.

We all have our priorities, and that's fine. But beekeeping is expensive to initiate. Yeah, there are places to save money, such as buying used equipment or making the equipment yourself. Despite the initial cost, I tell beginners the best thing to do is start out by buying new equipment. See how it goes together and how it functions. Then you can begin to work on making your own equipment if you are so inclined.

If you were to ask the members of a bee club, buying used equipment is highly frowned upon. These seasoned experts will cite disease, namely American Foul Brood (often abbreviated, AFB). I confess much of my beginning beekeeping was built on used equipment. I didn't have any disease issues. Maybe I was lucky. If there was a downside, this used equipment rotted a whole lot sooner, but I felt I got my money's worth, but only in the short run.

Yes, you can make your own equipment, but I find the quality of the wood at most lumber yards just as expensive as the pre-cut, exact-measurement of the wood I can buy from the beekeeping supply house. If I can find free scrap wood, I'll build my own. If you do, make sure every measurement fits the Langstroth conventions.

<u>Where There's a Will, There's a Way</u>:

I got my start in beekeeping with some money I saved through my college years.

Years later, as I wanted to expand and I had a wife and three small children under the age of five, I found myself scrounging in dumpsters for junked pallets. I pirated and cannibalized packing crates and cut out my own equipment.

Soon after that I was pricing used equipment and placing classified want-ads in the local newspapers looking for used beekeeping equipment. A lot of those purchases were nothing but worn out hives masquerading as high-grade kindling material.

Back in those days I had more time than money. It goes to show you can get started on a shoe-string budget rather than buying new equipment at new prices. But I also owned a table saw and possessed a rather crude ability for wood working.

But it also goes to demonstrate that the will is more powerful than the wallet. If you really want to get started keeping bees, don't let the financial investment put you off. Think of the expense of starting as an investment that will pay future dividends. Think of a bee hive as a goose that lays golden eggs…really running, sticky golden eggs we call honey.

And if that were true, how much would you pay for that goose? How many of these geese do you want to place in your barn? That's the philosophy that moved me to purchase twenty nucs to get started. I possessed great boldness and that wild dream of harvesting baskets of those golden eggs. But then again, in 1981, these hives didn't cost $375 each!

And I had a vision of what I wanted to achieve.

How many hives makes a good start? Two hives are recommended to start. Why two hives when you can only afford one? Two hives will give you a wonderful comparison between the two hives. One will be stronger than the other and if one should die, you can make a split (there I go again with the jargon) and repopulate the dead hive.

I think four hives is better than two when starting out. But when you start doing the math, four hives is a sizeable investment. Six hives would give you an even better comparison, but again, we're talking about a lot of money.

Sometimes you need to jump in over your head to learn how to swim. Once you get going, you can always expand by making your own splits from your own hives which will reduce the investment costs of expansion. Once you get going, you can see how simple these bee boxes really are and make some for yourself.

Just don't get caught in the "paralysis of analysis" waiting for that magical day when everything will work out. Life is full of risks and if you wait until everything is right, you'll never get started.

Making the Initial Move:

One of the first questions I'm asked is, "Can you help me get started?" The answer is, "Yes, I can." But you will still have to do most of the work and you'll have to take responsibility for observing the day-to-day changes. I can only hold your hand for so long before I cut you loose to sail on your own. But I'm more than willing to help you get started.

The second question is almost always, "How much does it cost to get started?" When I quote the figures I gave above, I'm met with incredulous, mouth-gaping, blank stares. Yes, it's expensive to get started. Yes, there are cheaper alternatives to getting started like buying used equipment, but for the beginner beekeeper, it's best to start with brand new equipment until you understand how it works.

I find it disheartening that it costs so much to get started. Some potential beekeepers have to first convince their spouse this money is a good investment. But you have to realize this is not something you can jump into today and decide to get out next week. This is a commitment. It's an investment.

There will be dividends for those who stick with it. It's not a get rich quick scheme, though I think it has tremendous potential to "adequately" compensate your efforts over the long run. There will be some annual expenses. You have to feed that goose some grain to get the golden eggs...and you'll eventually need to find someone to buy those golden eggs.

But people get started in beekeeping every day and make a success of it. You can, too!

There are two things you need to do at this point. First, you need to decide if you're going to do it. Are you going to keep bees? Are you ready to make the commitment?

Remember what Yoda said in the Star Wars movie: *"Do, or not do. There is no try."*

Make up your mind you're going to do it. Make up your mind you're going to succeed.

But the second thing to do at this point is to determine your purpose for keeping bees. Your success is closely linked to your purpose. When you know your purpose you will have vision. Having a vision of what you want to accomplish, of where you want to go, gives you direction.

I make no apologies when I tell people I keep bees to make honey and I sell honey to make money. That's my bottom line. That's my purpose that fuels my vision.

When I think of the honey the bees will produce, I find a lot of patience in dealing with the stings. When I think of the money that honey translates into, I develop a great tolerance for the heat and humidity of a Missouri summer as I lug those heavy boxes brim full with honey. I make no complaints about buying new equipment because I have seen what the bees can accomplish.

You need to decide why you're willing to invest the money, the time and the energy and endure the stings. When you know your purpose you'll develop a vision for beekeeping and forbearance for the sacrifices it takes.

Yes, I firmly believe in counting the cost before building, but somewhere along the planning stages, you're going to find yourself facing an open door. You'll ponder if you should step through the threshold. You hesitate looking for more information about this open door.

But at some stage you're just going to have to take a step of faith, pony up the money and make the investment. There will no doubt be a lot of questions, especially from your spouse. But like everything else, the first step is always the hardest. After the first step, momentum begins to propel you forward.

Purpose Defines Vision:

So why are you interested in keeping bees? Do you have a purpose or a reason for investing so much money in equipment? Can you explain to a spouse or a friend why this hobby makes sense? It won't make any sense to most people.

And bear in mind, as I sit down to write this manuscript, I'm happy for your interest in keeping bees. Really, I'm glad for your curiosity in a hobby that is best known for two things: stinging insects and honey...the worst and the best reasons to keep bees. But most people see the former as too painful to acquire the latter.

We need more beekeepers in the United States, no question. When asked if the bees are still dying, I respond with a qualified, "Yes." However, one of our problems is our beekeepers are dying. Commercial beekeepers are aging and retiring faster than we can find younger replacements. Young people are simply not picking up the call to keep bees.

I'd like to see you get some bees and have a great time learning about this wonderful insect. I wish for your success. I hope you have a magnificent experience. I expect you're going to be keeping bees for a long time. The blessings and benefits are worth the stings and hard work, plus you're doing the world a favor by keeping bees. You're helping our food supply and producing a wonderful, health-filled treat.

What I want to do is move you forward with an eyes-wide-open reality. You need to know that this is a complicated time to keep bees. Pesticides and pollution are increasing and proving to be an ever-present threat to the bees. I find it somewhat ironic, following all the media hype of CCD, (Colony Collapse Disorder, known to many as "that mysterious diseases that's killing our bees"), how this honey bee crisis has inspired a virtual army of beekeeping soldiers willing to move directly to the front lines where the battle rages at its worst. You are to be commended, but be aware: there will be casualties. I don't want you to be one of them.

And it's not that I think your bees will succumb to CCD. But pesticides are on the increase. As the bugs that plague our food crops increase, so does the need for harsher, stronger chemicals to combat them.

Every year there's a new pest, calling for a better chemical that kills stronger pests. Then we have a resistance developing in our pests so we are forced to apply twice as much. Honeybees are caught in the cross-fire.

It's also a challenging time as the pastures and fence rows that once supported clover and wild flowers are being plowed under in favor of corn. Corn is not a nectar-producing crop.

Additionally, the crops that support honeybees are now being cultivated in genetically modified forms, sometimes written as GMO crops. Some of these GMO crops do not secrete nectar, and if there is no nectar, there will be no honey produced.

I cannot honestly confirm all GMO crops are bad or hazardous for human consumption. There are no tests that have proven GMO crops cause cancer or birth defects. But there is an incredible, public hysteria concerning suspicions that GMO crops cannot be good.

In reality, GMO crops require fewer pesticides because they have the good stuff to combat pests built into their DNA, their genetic code. But messing around with their genetics brings out our paranoia.

It's a challenging time to keep honeybees, let alone trying to start into this endeavor as a hobbyist.

The best defense against these challenges is to have a sense of vision. If you want to keep a couple of hives in the back yard to pollinate the garden, that's great. If you are thinking of keeping a large number of hives to make money selling honey, you will approach beekeeping with a different attitude and a different arsenal of management practices.

And your vision may change over the years or even your first year. But a sense of why you are entering this hobby or profession is best articulated in order to meet the challenges head-on.

Challenging Times:

This is a complicated time to start keeping bees, and it's especially challenging if you've never done it before. It's really challenging if you have no exposure or experience to the art and science of keeping bees. It can be extremely demanding if you have no tolerance to the heavy lifting during the hottest months of the year and the incessant stings. It's hard work.

But on the other hand, there are people like me who still remember the good old days when keeping bees was simple and easy. Back in those days, you could put bees in a box, set them on autopilot and come back in a month and harvest honey.

It's not that way anymore. Parasitic mites and increased usage of pesticides challenge the bees and those who keep them. There is still a contingent of old beekeepers who remember the "good old days."

Perhaps your lack of knowledge is good thing. I still try and get by on what we did forty years ago before varroa mites. I try and keep honeybees naturally and as chemical-free as possible. But even the locations where I keep bees is polluted with chemicals and it's beyond my control.

While you may not know much, at least you're not pining for the good old days when it was easy and not so complicated. The rest of us just have to get used to the fact that the old days aren't coming back. We need to look to the future. We need to make adjustments.

The people wanting to start keeping bees to help the bees survive CCD are to be commended. But beekeeping is a whole lot more complicated than it used to be.

Still, it is ironic how the Alar chemical scare back in the late 1980s did not prompt people to start growing apple orchards. I find it amusing how the Mad Cow Disease of the late 1990s didn't inspire people to keep a calf in their backyard. When the lead paint in children's toys made in China raised a raucous recall, no one I knew thought they would open a Toys-R-Us store. And yet, as the precious honey bee was threatened by this mysterious die-off we call CCD, the interest in keeping bees exploded exponentially. And these efforts are noble, but also a little naive.

Even today with the housing crisis, the credit crunch and the falling stock market, I don't see people clambering to get their real estate license, start lending money or open a stock brokerage office. And while the experts claim our economy is on the rebound, there is still much fear and trembling…except when it comes to taking up the mantle of beekeeping. And for this, I'm glad!

So what is the difference in people that inspires them to start keeping bees in a time when most beekeepers are being wiped out along with the honeybees? What is it that nudges people who know very little about this insect to want to get a boxful for their back yard?

Truthfully, I just don't know. But I while I wish you all the luck in the world, I want you to be fully aware these are trepid and insidious times. Some people are making a go of it, but it's hard sledding and an uphill battle. The going is tough, and many of the tough folks are opting to do something else. I want you to enter into this endeavor with your eyes wide open.

Beekeeping is a wonderful endeavor and the bees are incredibly fascinating. But this is an enterprise that takes a sizable investment of money and time, and it can be very rewarding, both financially and otherwise. But it's challenging.

And I don't want to sound negative. I just want you to enter with a realistic spirit of what you can expect and what is expected of you. I've known many one-season beekeepers who bought a bunch of equipment, bought a number of packages of bees, only to have their bees die the following winter. It didn't take much to force these sincere beekeepers to give up all hope. They quietly advertised their equipment for sale the following spring.

So if this is happens to you, if horrible die-offs became your situation, do you give up or plunk down more money for more bees the next spring? What do you tell your spouse who was already counting on some honey for Christmas gifts to the in-laws? How do you justify more money invested where previous plans have failed? And what if they die as well? The education of a beekeeper is expensive and the tuition is costly.

The Power of Perseverance:

Do you have the persistence to persevere? Successful beekeepers are resilient. Honeybees have proven themselves to be resilient. Will you be as resilient?

Having a purpose that develops your vision will help a great deal. And beekeeping is like any other business or hobby. I friend of mine had a female chocolate Labrador retriever. She bought this dog as a puppy for $500 (back when chocolate Labradors were all the rage). It came from a litter of nine pups so she does the math and figures she can breed her dog and make $4,500 selling nine puppies at $500 each pretty easy.

Even before the dog was bred, let alone old enough to be bred, she dreamed of making a down payment on a new truck on the money she'd make from selling puppies. This is vision. She had purpose. This is all good stuff!

Well, along the way to reaching breeding age, there were a number of trips to the veterinarian to maintain the dog's good health. There was a special diet that required expensive dog food. When she wanted to take a vacation, she paid to have the dog kenneled. Then she discovered the breeding fee also required her dog be kenneled at the stud breeder's place. All of these expenses were adding up. But vision kept her going. She had purpose. Not many people are ready to follow this path to their dreams.

The short end of this story is that she paid quite a sum to get the dog bred to a purebred stud. The puppies were born, actually numbering twelve pups, but a disease called Parvovirus killed them all. She had to start the breeding cycle over which meant more expenses without any income to show for it. A lesser person may have given up, but she had purpose and vision. She had the power to persevere.

She entered the world of raising puppies with her eyes dreamily closed. Then she was rudely awakened. I can only hope to give you enough encouragement to be ready for the normally tough challenges that face all of us. Just don't let me sound too negative. But allow me to shake you from any dreamy slumber that thinks beekeeping is a smooth road to vast riches. I firmly believe there is money to be made in keeping bees, but don't count your eggs before they hatch.

The roadway to bee keeping success is littered with the naïve intentions of those who thought bee keeping was easy. They dreamed of the romance associated with the nobility of environmentalism and green living. They thought all you had to do was put bees in a box and the honey would flow like a river.

And pricing jars of honey at the farmers market only whetted their appetite for the money they'd be making selling honey. They dreamed of people lining up at their front door just to get a jar of their honey. If only it were this easy.

I knew a one-season beekeeper whose bees died after his first year. He was discouraged, naturally, but held his resolve that he would be a beekeeper. But life brought him another opportunity. He put all his boxes in the garage, hoping to "get back into bees one of these days."

After five seasons of hopefully wishing, he asked me to come out and take the equipment off his hands. He gave me an offer of 25% of what he paid for it brand new. So we got out the supply catalog and started noting prices. And this equipment was just like new. The only down-side was I had to take it all. He had grown so discouraged he wanted the whole pile of equipment gone. He didn't even want a memory of what he thought he wanted lingering in his garage.

Unless you can find another beekeeper, the market for used (even one-season, almost new) equipment is just about zero. The equipment doesn't translate to another vocation. It is specific to beekeeping. Make sure you really want to get into this hobby as it may take more money than you realize, and it may be harder to recoup your investment costs if you decide to back out.

The Secret to Vision is Purpose:

What is your purpose in keeping bees? In all honesty, you may not know, at least not yet, and that's okay. Some people enter beekeeping because it really is a fascinating hobby. After a season or two, they discover you can harvest a nice crop of honey and sell it at the farmer's market or to your neighbors for a considerable amount of money.

That's when vision starts to come into focus.

When I take a phone call and the caller asks, "Can you help me get started in bees?" my first response is typically, "Sure." Then I follow up with a question of my own, "So why do you want to start keeping bees?"

Most of my callers tell me they just want to "play with some bees." Some say they just want to "have them around." Some mention "research" in their inquiry, as in CCD research, but I think this is something left up to the professionals. A number of people want to "save the honey bee" as honey bees are dying and they believe it is possible for someone with no experience and less knowledge to be the savior of the industry.

Others will mention the pollination of the garden and honey to give as Christmas presents. Still, there are some who feel the great salvation of the honey bees lies in the hands of the small, hobbyist beekeepers and they want to be part of this movement.

For what it will cost you to get into this "playing around," you may find it cheaper to do something else like stamp collecting. And at worst, with stamp collecting, you may end up with a paper cut. Bees sting and just about everyone in the universe feels compelled to tell me how they are allergic to bee stings. And if you change your mind and want to exit the hobby, selling stamps is easier than selling used bee equipment.

Richard Taylor, a phenomenal beekeeper and philosopher who is now deceased, compared rookie beekeepers to comets. He noted how new beekeepers excitedly buy equipment and get some bees, and every conversation they have focuses around their bees. Like a comet in the night sky, they streak brightly, standing out for the entire world to see, illuminating the skies with their excitement and enthusiasm.

But then something happens. Their bees die or they become a victim to a short-attention span. Or their spouse tells them that no more money is to be spent on another package of "those bees that are just going to die." They take on another hobby and what was once their brilliant bee keeping comet streaking across the night sky suddenly goes, "poof," and burns out.

Like most comets, what was once very a bright presence simply disappears without a trace. The next time you see them they won't even bring up the topic about beekeeping. Even if you ask, they'll change the subject to another topic of discussion.

And that's the last anyone ever hears of these beekeepers. They are on to something else. They hope this something else will pay for the money they lost in their beekeeping hobby. And it's too bad. Sometimes you have to give it one more try, but how many years of giving it "one more try" do you do? How patient is your spouse? How deep is your financial pocket?

The death of the biblical character Moses is described in the last chapter of Deuteronomy in the Old Testament. It says, in the New Revised Standard Version, that his eyesight was "undimmed" and his vigor was "unabated." It also says he was 120 years old.

Now I take that story at face value. He's an old man. But he still has that "fire in the belly." He still has his passion. That's what I hope for beekeepers, especially the new rookies but also for the seasoned veterans. I hope for a long and prosperous, rich and rewarding experience. I know if you're willing to keep at it, if your vision will stay undimmed and your ambitions remain unabated, you are ready for a wonderful time keeping bees.

But do not enter lightly. It will be work. There will be casualties.

Discovering Your Purpose:

I still hold to my original vision of a maintaining a profitable beekeeping enterprise. That's why I'm still keeping honeybees today. I maintain a vision that is undimmed. I keep bees to produce honey, which in turn, I sell to make money.

I manage my bees for maximum honey production and I published a book called, *A Ton of Honey: Managing Your Hives for Maximum Production*. In it, I wrote down all my secrets, tips and tricks to harvesting a literal ton of honey. You can view the details of that book at **http://maxhoney.homestead.com** or search my www.CreateSpace.com account as it will be posted in the near future.

I also wrote another book called, *Beekeeping with Twenty-five Hives: an in-depth look moving from the hobby level to becoming the profitable side-liner*. You can find that book at **http://25hives.homestead.com** or likewise, search my account or name at www.CreateSpace.com.

But let me get back to my purpose. My purpose in keeping bees fuels my vision. Vision ignites passion. I'm excited about keeping bees. I derive a great deal of satisfaction and joy from beekeeping. I also generate quite a bit of money.

Now on one hand, people are quick to point out to me the idea that "money is the root of evil." And they think, that as a Presbyterian preacher, I ought to know that verse from the Bible, and in some way, take a more humble, more frugal approach to my beekeeping.

Well, for starters, they have a partial knowledge of that verse (1 Timothy 6:10). It is the <u>LOVE</u> of money (not money itself) that is <u>A</u> root of all kinds of evil (there are obvious many different roots and various kinds of evil). Money, in and of itself, is not bad. It's what it does to us or drives us to do that creates evil. But by itself, money is just a tool, a measurement of our success.

The money from my beekeeping business has been a source of additional income for extra expenses for my family. It's a sideline. It's an income-producing hobby (though my wife calls it a "hobby on steroids"). There's nothing wrong with making money selling honey.

So what is your purpose in keeping bees? Why do you want to get started? What plans do you have? What's your motivation?

Defining your purpose will be invaluable, in the long run. But you may not be able to articulate a short-term, first year plan other than getting a couple of hives.

I encourage you to begin to think of long-term plans and a greater purpose. Surely these plans are subject to change, as mine have been, but you have to start somewhere. When you decide to start, it becomes a place where you can expand and grow into different areas. But everyone has to start somewhere.

Making a Living Keeping Honeybees:

After people feel me out with some basic questions about getting started, the real question becomes: Can you make money, enough money to live on keeping honey bees? Could it become your sole source of income?

This question shows a longer-term point of view. It begins to shape your purpose or at least shows you are thinking of a purpose. From purpose, you can start making plans.

The answer to this real question is, "Yes!" But you have to intentionally manage your bees for maximum honey production and you have to enjoy marketing your honey and you have to have enough hives to have enough honey to market consistently to your customers or your wholesale outlets. So it's really a qualified, "yes," but a very probable possibility.

One of my beekeeping buddies was having a hard time keeping his bees alive through the winter. He bought a bunch of used beekeeping equipment, bought some packages of bees and installed them. During the summer, they did quite nicely. But then they all died during the winter. This is not uncommon.

So the next spring, he buys more bees. For some reason, those bees die out the following winter. Again, nothing too unusual about this scenario though he chose a specific management track that made it more difficult for this bees to survive. So the following spring, as before, he spends more money buying new packages of bees to replace the dead bees that died during the winter. It's the same story on his winter losses and he spends more money buying new bees. And note, he has yet to harvest any honey as first-year package bees installed into a hive seldom make any honey.

In one of the bee meetings he prophetically announced, "There's no money in beekeeping!"

To which his wife sarcastically replied, "Not the way you keep them!"

Is there money in bees? Yes, there is! But you have to manage your hives accordingly. You need to manage your bees for survival. Should you go into beekeeping with dollar signs in your eyes? Not necessarily, but if you want to make money in keeping bees, then you need to set your vision for this purpose. If this is your purpose, you need to make the right plans to fulfill this purpose.

For all we could tell, this beekeeper was just keeping bees for the fun of it, but having your bees die is not fun. Buying new bees every spring is not fun, either.

Now if you just want a hive in the back yard, a hive you keep just to mess around with in your spare time, you may not harvest very much honey. But then again, if putting in the work and maximizing your honey harvest is not your purpose, messing around with one hive in the back yard when you have some free time is a perfectly acceptable way to keep bees.

Everyone keeps bees for different reasons and all of these reasons are valid. I compare it to keeping dogs. I know some dog owners who have their dogs highly trained for hunting. Some dog owners teach their dogs tricks. My dog? Well, my dog Dusty isn't too bright. We don't work with her to fetch. She really only behaves when you have some article of food. She doesn't hunt. Mostly, she lays around the yard and barks at strangers. She is a very loving dog.

But my plans and purposes for having this mixed-breed "mutt" are different than other dog owners. Different purposes doesn't make one dog owner better than the other.

And getting back to beekeeping, I don't think your purpose is necessarily set in stone. Things change. I've known some older beekeepers who wanted to make money with their honey and they started out with that specific purpose. That was their vision. They watched me sell honey at the farmers market and they wanted in on a piece of that action. They wanted a slice of the pie. Unfortunately, I made it look easy.

So I helped them get started with a couple of colonies of bees. Then they found out how heavy these boxes are when filled with honey. And they complained how hot and humid the weather was in the summer, and more so when they dressed up in their bees suits because they didn't like getting stung.

And when you go to harvest your honey, the bees are more than a little reluctant to hand it over to you. Then these older beekeepers found out no one came busting down their door when they let people know they had local honey for sale. They didn't have their market established and they didn't have the patience to build a client base.

So they revised their purpose and now keep bees for fun and work their bees when they want to, not when they have to according to their previous purpose.

Another beekeeping buddy of mine switched from honey production to honey bee removal from buildings and structures. He doesn't care if he produces one drop of honey, but he found his real joy was working with homeowners who had honey bees move into their buildings. And he charges money to remove the bees. He also has the skill to repair what he tears apart. Removing bees became his purpose, and it provides a pretty nice income for him.

So there are different reasons to keep bees. And it's okay to revise your plans and seek a different purpose. We all do it every day in the different aspects of our life. But somewhere you're going to decide to make a start, someday you're going to make the investment despite having imperfect knowledge of this craft. It will be a step of faith.

And remember an important item: There are things you cannot know and things you can only learn by jumping in over your head. I encourage you to go for it.

Keep something else in mind: If you wait until you have perfect knowledge and know, for sure, that everything will work out, you'll never get started.

But start with a purpose in mind. Start with a vision of where you want this hobby to take you. Yes, it can provide an income sufficient to support a nice lifestyle. Yes, it can be a lot of fun. The most important thing is to get started and see where this fascinating hobby will take you.

Books and Resources:

Okay, so you've made up your mind you want to keep bees. You've convinced yourself and your spouse that keeping bees is what you want to do and you've promised yourself that you're going to give it the necessary attention it needs to be a success.

Further, you've given some thought as to why you want to keep bees. You've articulated a purpose. You have a vision of where you want to go.

Now what?

You need to arm yourself with the mental resources and intellectual ammunition to enter the fray. And so as people come up to me and begin to converse about keeping bees, I next ask them, "How many beekeeping books have you read?"

Sadly, hardly anyone has read anything. The only thing that has caught their eye is the doom-and-gloom stories hyped in various media outlets on how our bees and dying and we're all going to starve in three years.

Three years? Yes. Some guy named "Einstein" (yeah, really) is quoted as saying that if the bees all die the human race will starve in three years.

I'm sure you've heard the quote, but don't be fooled into thinking "Albert" Einstein said it. No one really knows where it came from, or if it was truly, actually said. And no one knows who this Einstein was. It might have been his cousin, Roscoe Einstein.

In truth, our American diet is made up of corn, potatoes, rice and wheat—none of which require pollination by insects. We're not going to starve if the bees all died. Unfortunately, the loss of honeybees as pollinators would mean the demise of many of our specialty crops, fruits and vegetables.

However, this news of humanity's demise (by starvation) is all some people have read and they want to start keeping bees in order to help the situation and possibly save the honeybee.

I admire their rationale, though sometimes I wonder if they want to keep bees thinking it will keep them from starving. However, the world needs more beekeepers and we need more bees. But we're not going to starve.

Like many of these people, you are likely and likewise moved by our plight of the disappearing bee. But as I said earlier, these are complicated times. Keeping honey bees is not what it used to be. You need to stay up to speed on the most current developments.

So I ask these prospective beekeepers how many books they have read. Almost all the time, no one has read anything except the stories in the newspapers concerning the supposed shortage of honey bees. And they don't really read the newspapers beyond the headline. Personally, I think the bee crisis is over-hyped.

And even the validity of that coverage is suspect, but that's a greater digression I don't have time to get into.

So on the topic of how many books you should read on beekeeping, let me give you two quotes.

> *"The average person only reads one book a year.*
> *That's why they're average."*

> *"The person who has a book but does not read it*
> *is no better off than the person who cannot read."*

You will reap huge benefits if you read all the books you can read on beekeeping. And aside from books on beekeeping, what's the last book you did read? How many books have you read in the last year?

Sadly, most people don't read anything, not even the newspaper. We are a nation of non-readers. We watch the boob-tube as mindless drivel streams in front of our eye-balls in the form of survivor/elimination contests and reality shows. But challenging our minds with something we read seems like too much work.

Knowledge is power. Empower yourself with information.

Books:

For most people, reading is a lost art, a neglected mental exercise that has us wasting our brains away. I blame television that tells us what we need to believe (often mis-labeled as the "news") and colors our world and distorts our reality (so-called "reality" shows that are nothing but fluff and fantasy and contrived situations with scripted conversations to bring out the worst side of people).

I think of the mindless drivel that passes for these 24-hour "news" channels. Humanity is slowly dying from ignorance and spoon-fed opinions in a ratings race to capture more viewership. Go into any doctor's office, barbershop, fast food restaurant and anywhere a television is on and the channel is almost always on these "news" shows. Remember when restaurants didn't have to have televisions to occupy our time?

How many of us actually read the newspaper, other than perhaps those who read the obituaries, the comics and the sports section?

I'm going to challenge you to get some books and read about keeping bees. Now here is some good news. The bees know what to do. You don't have to train them to forage for nectar. The bees don't have to take classes on turning nectar into honey or the proper way to feed their larvae. They know this stuff. But you need to know as well.

Your knowledge of honey bee biology will affect your management. You have to know what the bees are doing so you know what you need to do, and what you do is governed by your purpose. Or like that husband I quoted in a previous chapter, you can buy new packages of bees every spring and complain there is no money in beekeeping. Your choice.

Find some good books to read. Heck, even reading some bad books will help. But the idea is to keep reading and keep filling your mind with information on keeping honeybees.

Books Cost Money:

Where to start? My suggestion is to visit your local library. Most public libraries have some books on bees and beekeeping. They may also have some books on homesteading or gardening that may have chapters on bees. I suggest you check them all out.

But there are two downsides to visiting your public library. The first downside is most people in the general public don't have a library card. But this is no problem. Apply and get one. Most times they're free.

And along these lines, most people can't navigate their way around the library and they think the Dewey Decimal System is something to measure the weather. So suck up your pride and ask the librarian for help. They are very helpful and most of them are kind of pretty.

The second downside is that the beekeeping books in most public libraries are old books from the 1970s and 1980s. And sadly, they won't have many books to start with, but the library is a free resource and an ideal place for you to start.

Here's some good news: certain things with the bees have not changed. It still takes twenty-one days for a bee egg to hatch into an adult bee. Bees still gather nectar. Bees still die when they sting you. Most of the "technology" we incorporate into our modern practices were developed by a Congregational Pastor named Lorenzo Langstroth in the 1860s. Don't let the antiquity of these books fool you. Read them. It's free information. And the librarians are fun to flirt with.

There are many things that have not changed in the life of the beekeeper. That's the good news of reading the free books from the public library. But there are many brand-new challenges that won't be in those old library books. You won't find anything on mites or the influx of Africanized bees. You won't find anything on the small hive beetle, or the large hive beetle for that matter. Colony Collapse Disorder is a recent media development and I'd be happily surprised if anything will be covered in any of your local library books.

You may ask your librarian to do an "inter-library" loan and request some modern books, and my local library has a computer that will pull up and locate books in seven different branches. Sometimes a local library will do searches across the country and procure those books for you, free of charge in most cases. Hopefully, with the influx of new beekeepers and the increased exposure on most media outlets with the disappearing bee stories, your local library will have at least thought to get a modern book on beekeeping.

But the reality is most libraries have limited budgets for new acquisitions and beekeeping is just not the highest subject on the librarian's wish list. Beekeeping, despite its resurgence in the past few years, is still a hobby of a minority of the public. Librarians run public institutions that cater to a wider audience. One of the things I've done is to buy new books on beekeeping which I've donated to the public library after I've read them. This is about the only way our local library is going to stay current on the topic of beekeeping.

So after reading your local library fare of antiquated books, ask the librarian to find some modern books. But I can almost guarantee that task won't take long. Libraries just don't keep up to date on beekeeping books. Or visit your favorite retail bookseller like Barnes and Nobles and buy the new books. But don't spend too much time searching the shelves of the brick-and-mortar store. Their selection of books on beekeeping serves a minority, and like libraries, they cater to a larger audience.

However, they have computers and access to new releases. Request a book and most stores will gladly order it for you, but don't count on them having it in stock. The demand just doesn't warrant them carrying these kinds of books on their shelves.

Books are expensive, however. You may do better searching the Internet for discount sites like Amazon.com for books on beekeeping. There will be shipping charges that offset any discounts. If you're not computer savvy, ask your teen-age daughter for help. I do.

Check the auction site, ebay.com for beekeeping books. But don't be fooled by the reprinted books they market as "new." They are old books where the copyright has run out and the book entered the public domain for anybody to reprint. It's the "condition" of the book that's new, not the subject matter. And most of these books are older than the library books you can borrow for free.

Two contemporary and modern books I like are *The Backyard Beekeeper* by Kim Flottum and *Beekeeping for Dummies* by Howland Blackiston. Both are written for the new beekeeper who only wants to keep a few hives.

And if you should come across any book by Sue Hubbell, buy it. Sue writes differently, almost poetically and philosophically. Her lessons in beekeeping come in a narrative fashion and the learning process is intuitive. And every day there are more books published. All you have to do is ask the clerk at the retail book store to search the list of new releases and they'll do the work for you.

Here's some more good news: You don't have to buy a whole bookshelf of books. The previously two mentioned books will cover the gamut and span the spectrum of what you need to know. Sue's books will fill in the gaps. And she's a very engaging writer.

But read. If you don't read, you're no better off than the person who can't read. And if you don't read, then you set yourself to the mercy of the news media. My thoughts on watching the news is don't believe everything they say. Everyone has an agenda.

If you attend any beginner classes on beekeeping, those people will have their choices and selections. Most classes recommend two books, *The ABC's and XYZ's of Beekeeping* and *The Hive and the Honeybee*. Both of these books are thick and exhaustive. Buy them if you want, but if this is your first year, they may be a bit much. You may find them overwhelming. They are weighty tomes.

And if you buy them from the retail bookseller or off the Internet, these particular two books are very expensive. But they are also very good and well worth the money. If you continue into your second or third year of keeping bees, they may be a fine investment. So if you're in this hobby for the long haul, they are very good. They are research-level, top-drawer material and they are revised every other year.

Magazines:

There are two magazines that I would like you to read. Most beekeepers subscribe to these magazines and each one seems to cater to special interests and different levels of experience. What I find is some beekeepers prefer one over the other.

The first magazine is called, "Bee Culture." It is written more to the level of the smaller, hobbyist beekeepers and the articles are written more to the beginner. Write or call and they'll send you a free sample.

Bee Culture 800-289-7668

http://www.beeculture.com

The second magazine, "American Bee Journal," is a little more advanced and contains research articles and global beekeeping experiences in foreign countries. Likewise, call or write and they'll send you a free sample.

American Bee Journal 271-847-3324

http://www.americanbeejournal.com

I've written articles published in both magazines and I subscribe to both of them. There was a time one of my beekeeping buddies subscribed to Bee Culture and I subscribed to the American Bee Journal. Then each month we swapped magazines and we read the other magazine without paying for a subscription. If you join a local bee club, encourage the club to buy a subscription that you can all share.

These magazines cost money for subscriptions, but I think they are well worth it. First, you get the most up-to-date news and information about the beekeeping industry. Second, you expose yourself to advertisers and manufacturers of equipment.

As a beginner, I think I would opt to Bee Culture as the preferred magazine of the two, but if you can afford it, subscribe to both or talk a buddy into buying a subscription for the other one. Or tell your spouse you want a subscription for your birthday.

It may not be such a good idea to suggest a subscription for your anniversary…unless your spouse is also interested in beekeeping.

Internet Access:

The Internet offers some of the most current news and information. It also contains a lot of opinions and fraudulent offers to increase the size of your earlobes (or other body parts, for that matter), offers of the latest weight-loss herbal supplement, and of course, finding true love and saving hundreds of dollars by refinancing your mortgage for your time-share in Gulf Shores.

There are also some incredibly lucrative offers from Nigerian royalty that will make me a millionaire that I have yet to take advantage of!

But there is also a host of good information. Simply get on any good search engine like **www.google.com** (my favorite) or **www.yahoo.com** (my second choice) and simply type in phrases and words like "beginning beekeeping."

You'll be inundated with thousands of websites, and don't be surprised or feign some kind of shock when some of these Internet searches leads you to something pornographic. It's out there. And even the innocent searches like merely typing, "queen honey bee," into your web's search engine can just about guarantee a porn site in the first ten listings.

It's quite overwhelming..all the name of free speech. Ah, the Internet is a wonderful thing and it's a annoying thing.

There is one really good web site that functions like an electronic bulletin board service, sometimes confused with "chat rooms." This site, **www.beesource.com**, can be viewed without giving up any personal information. It's free. It's moderated to keep the spam out of the legitimate conversations. If you just want to read the responses, you're called a "lurker" and lurking is welcome.

But if you want to join in the conversation and "post" a comment, you'll be asked for some personal information and you can choose a "log-in" name. You will also give them a password of your choosing. This bulletin board functions as a discussion group, and after you log in, you can enter your questions and offer responses to the topics of discussion. And to join in on the conversation is still free.

If you have problems with logging in or coming up with a log-in name or password, ask your teen-age daughter. Or better yet, ask my daughter. She knows how to navigate the Internet with blinding speed and agility. Somewhere the computer genes fell to her and she's a computer whiz. Or maybe I'm still an old fart. I'm still stuck in the year of yellow legal pads and ball-point pens.

This forum, beesource, is great for asking questions and listening to what others are doing. If there is a downside, many of the people posting questions and responses use "bee talk," a specific jargon that incorporates words like "nucs" and SHB and FWIW and AFAIK.

But the more you read, the more you'll start catching on. And you'll also find a host of competing and conflicting opinions. And that's what they are: opinions. But listening to other's opinions is still of benefit. Read everything with a grain of salt.

And don't be upset if someone disagrees with your opinion. The Internet is purposefully anonymous, and some people hide behind fake names just for the purpose of "flaming" (disagreeing in a discourteous manner) another opinion.

To sum up this section, if you really want to raise bees, you're going to have to do a little reading. Reading will open the door so you can have an intelligent conversation. Otherwise, when someone explains something, it will be like a foreign language. Read and you'll familiarize yourself with the language.

Equipment:

Okay, let's broach the subject about equipment. First off, remember how I begged you to subscribe to Bee Culture and the American Bee Journal? These magazines are your best bets for finding suppliers of bee equipment as all the major players in the business of supplying bee equipment advertise in both magazines.

Here in the United States, we have standardized equipment called "Langstroth" hives. Almost every supplier has equipment standardized to these measurements. If you attend a bee club and they start talking about "Warre" hives and top bar hives (TBHs), you should know they are different and their management is different. Yes, you can make them work, but I strongly suggest you start with Langstroth, conventional hives. But that's just my opinion.

So look through the magazine and contact suppliers and request a catalog. Just about every supplier will send a free catalog. If you simply call for a free issue of each magazine, you'll have the best resource for finding most of the suppliers. Many of these suppliers also have web sites where you can request a catalog.

Ordering on-line, however, has been a challenge for me as websites and the "search" features are lacking for many of these suppliers. They ought to enlist the services of my daughter. She would get their shopping carts up to speed and much more user-friendly. However, if you search on the Internet, call for a catalog. My experience has proven that catalogs are easier to work with as opposed to on-line shopping and e-commerce shopping carts.

Catalogs are also great sources of information and inspiration. They will handle the latest trends (and fads) and the equipment you need to be part of the trend. They will also carry the latest chemicals and share instructions how these chemicals are to be applied.

One thing you will find: all of the catalogs will carry the same basic equipment, with the same basic, Langstroth measurements. Prices will vary, slightly. Shipping options will vary depending upon where you live. But one catalog will be like another, and I still enjoy reading every catalog I can get my hands on.

And like surfing the Internet for beginning beekeeping sites, you may be overwhelmed with all the options. The real difference between suppliers is with specialty items, branded items and shipping costs (which will vary depending upon their location).

I also find differences in customer service, especially when I'm talking to one of the order-takers on the phone or trying to navigate their on-line order form.

My initial advice is to call or write and request a catalog from all of them. Most of them have tips and advice, and even suggestions for a "beginner" set up kit. Unfortunately, the beginner kit will include a bunch of stuff you may not need. It may be cheaper to price the individual items, ala carte, rather than ordering a complete kit. Nevertheless, it will show you what's available and give you some ideas on what it costs to get into beekeeping.

The other value of reading these catalogs of supplies is it will give you a vocabulary. So when the bee club is talking about supers or medium frames, foundation or queen excluders, you'll have a pretty good idea of what those things look like. You may not have yet figured out what they are used for, but that's why you bought *Beekeeping for Dummies* and *The Backyard Beekeeper.*

If you've been stymied by the initial investment of buying bee equipment, I've priced some of the very basic, first-year equipment and came up with a rough figure of $150 per hive. That's the bare-bones minimum that will get you through the first year for each hive. You'll need to spend another $100 to finish out the required equipment for the next year. Shipping will be extra. In general, figure about $250 per hive for the equipment to get going and you can split that cost between your first two years establishing the colonies.

Sometimes it's easier to order it all at once, but some people just don't have the money for all the hives they want. So order what you need for this first year. Save your money and pick up what you need for the second year. You can also save on shipping through your local bee club if they pool orders or if someone is willing to drive and pick up the supplies.

If you want a bee suit, veil, gloves, smoker this will also cost more, probably in the neighborhood of another $100.

Bees are another expense and will cost around $125 per hive. Working with an experienced beekeeper through your local club or beekeeping association will lessen this cost.

When asked by prospective beekeepers, I shoot them a total figure of $350 to $375 per hive to get the hive up and running, filled with bees and prepared for honey production. But you may not produce honey your first year and buying only part of the equipment may be best for your personal budget.

If you want extracting equipment, that's another $500. So plan on expenses of a one-time cost of $600 plus $375 per each hive. But you may not necessarily need the extracting equipment the first year, and by all means, find a mentor who will tell you what you need and if they are in a generous frame of mind, they may even let you extract your honey at their place. A good mentor may be able to find some used equipment to help ease the cost of the initial start up.

So how many hives should you start out with? I would say a minimum of two, but four would be better. The reason you want more than one hive is that no hive is like another. One hive of those four will be very strong, two will be normal, and one hive will likely die out the first year. If you start with one hive, the hive that dies out may be the one you have.

Sounds horrible, but that's kind of the seasonal average. And in some cases, all four hives survive! Some years, all four hives die! You could get by with two hives, but I would definitely work on getting more than one hive.

At these prices, the topic of used equipment comes up, especially buying used equipment from me. I'm not picky as to my equipment and most of my equipment is in rough shape. But it works for the bees, so it works for me. I'm not picky.

And it's not for sale.

In a moment of generosity and kindness, I've sold some of my extra boxes and few bottom boards here and there to other aspiring beekeepers. It has always backfired on me. All I got was complaints. These prima donnas complained how rough and worn this old equipment was and how I charged too much for what I sold them.

I guess they thought I would sell them my very best equipment at bargain-basement prices. But what they didn't realize is that I didn't sell them my worst equipment either. I sold them fully functional, well-used equipment at very reasonable prices. Sometimes when they complained about financial hardship, I gave good equipment away for free. And they still complained. Complaints don't sit well with me.

This rough, used equipment works for me and my bees. But it gets back to my purpose: honey production. I'm not looking to make my apiary into a Martha Stewart, Award Winning Back Yard Apiary. I'm choosing function over form. And bear in mind, if I sell you some of my used equipment, I've got to find replacement pieces, likely new, at new prices. It's just easier for me to tell you to pay the big bucks up front and buy new equipment yourself. There's just a lot less complaining.

Secondarily, used equipment runs the risk of spreading disease. To be safe, many experts suggest you "scorch" or "torch" the inside of the hive bodies to sterilize them of any disease spores. It's a lot of extra work. But if you don't know the history of the equipment, or if the bee keeper cannot reasonably tell you how or why the bees which formerly occupied these hive bodies died, you run the risk of picking up a disease.

In my early days, I bought equipment at every deceased beekeeper's estate sale. I had retirees and widows give me used equipment. I never caught any diseases, but I spent a lot of time cleaning and repairing. And a lot of this equipment was short-lived.

After three seasons the corners were beginning to rot and the frames were breaking. What I really bought was simply pre-retirement beekeeping equipment. And I spent a good deal of time fixing and repairing and giving everything a fresh coat of paint. But it didn't give me the life-expectancy that I would have found with new equipment.

If I had to do it over again, I'd buy used equipment, but I'd lower my expectations. I'd use it and save money in the short-run, in order to buy new equipment to replace it for the long-run. I'd also be more judicious in choosing which pieces of used equipment I'd buy or I'd be better off walking away and simply saying, "no thanks."

If time is money, then I wasted a good deal of money fixing old stuff that had a short life span once I put bees in them. If there is an advantage to used equipment it will be the reduced price. I saved money on the shipping charges had I bought new equipment, and used equipment comes painted and assembled.

But I still spent quite a bit of time repairing and repainting. You can buy used equipment if you want. Finding it is harder than you would think. Once you make some money at your beekeeping enterprise (provided you plan on sticking around for the long-haul) you can buy new equipment. By the time you're ready for new equipment, this used equipment may be ready for retirement.

My best advice, however, is to order some new equipment and get set up. Once you know what you need and how things work, you can make your own equipment. And when you buy new equipment, you'll have a rough estimate on how to value used equipment.

In my early days, when I had more time than money, I could be found in the back alleys of restaurant supply companies and agricultural implement dealers salvaging packing crates and pallets. The wood was pine (very easy to utilize) and it was free.

If you go to the major retail lumber yards and buy what passes for the modern lumber yard (Lowes or Home Depot), you'll find over-priced wood of inferior quality. Additionally, you still have to cut it out. And you're going to pay for all the wood you cut away, the trimmings that you'll likely burn in the fireplace.

Go to the lumber yard and price what they're selling. Then take a look at your catalogs. Compare prices of the supplier's ready-to-assemble boxes to buying and sawing out store-bought pieces of lumber. You won't save much money, but you may have an enjoyable day working in your wood shop.

Besides, thinking I got something for nothing picking up scrap wood makes me feel good, and in my early days I had more time than money. I just could not afford to buy new equipment.

If you want to make your own equipment, I suggest you buy a set of boxes and bee hives from one of the major suppliers to get the exact measurements, then start cutting out boxes to those standard sizes. And don't deviate from the measurements. Measure twice and cut once. These are the standard measurements used in the industry.

I've tried to reinvent the wheel only to regret the decision later. There are plans for making your own equipment all over the Internet. And by all means, stick to the conventional "Langstroth" sizes.

In summary, I think used equipment is not worth the time to clean and repair, but depending on the source, it may be a cheap way to enter the beekeeping business. Most of the used equipment, depending on age and where it was stored, may have a short life in your apiary. But it may get you started inexpensively and you can start buying new equipment with the money you make selling honey.

If you can find scrap lumber for free, you can assemble most of your own equipment (I've never made the intricate frames) but your time commitment may offset any of the savings from the free lumber. However, the relaxing atmosphere in my wood shop makes this a viable alternative.

But in reality, buying ready-made, ready-to-assemble equipment is the best way. Everything is standard sized (for the most part with slight variations). All of the supply catalogs will have standardized equipment, and as you grow your interest in keeping bees, you will want everything standardized. That way, if you buy new or buy used, everything will be interchangeable.

I've bought some home-made equipment that wasn't standard. It seemed these old men who had a creative wood shop thought they were going to reinvent the wheel. But years ago, Rev. Langstroth went to work and designed what really works great for us today. Let's not mess it up!

In retrospect, when I've bought used equipment, it was an inefficient method of acquiring bee equipment. Further, when I bought estates, I had to buy the entire lot. I could not cherry-pick the good stuff and leave the rotted boxes for someone else.

After taking my purchase home, once I had thrown out the rotten, mice-chewed boxes and odd-sized, home-made boxes, I probably could have just as easily bought the new equipment I actually needed and be set. And I would not have spent the entire day at the auction or estate sale.

Let me quickly add two other thoughts. First, if you go to the catalogs and buy the "beginners" kit, it will have some stuff you don't necessarily need. But the real problem I have with beginner kits is the cost.

If you were to "piece-meal" the components and equipment you need and buy them separate, ala carte, the cost will be less even though you're still buying all the same components from the beginners kit. With the beginners kit you're paying for convenience and a one-stop shopping trip.

Second, and this is my problem with beginners kits, use wax foundation in your frames instead of plastic. This is highly critical, especially for package bees though not so much for nucs. Plastic foundation is a convenience for the beekeeper, but the bees are less enthused. Bees will balk at drawing out plastic foundation. Yet for some reason, the suppliers like to send out plastic foundation with their beginner kits. If at all possible, ask your supplier for wax foundation.

Not everyone has problems with plastic foundation, but so many beekeepers have complained to me that their bees failed to thrive that I was moved to write another resource on how to best manage plastic foundation. You'll find it with my other books (coming soon) or you can find it at:

http://www.makingplasticfoundationwork.homestead.com

And lastly, buy your equipment in the winter when you'll have time to assemble and paint. My initial venture into beekeeping was when

I bought nucs of bees and the equipment for the hives at the same time. Dumb. The hives were not assembled.

So I had to set out my nucs while I hurried up and assembled my equipment. Those nucs lost about five good days when they could have been growing. You want everything ready to go prior to receiving your bees. And that's the next chapter.

Acquiring Bees:

Everyone who talks to me thinks I am willing to sell them some bees. Most of my bees are working for me and the seasonality of beekeeping has my bees on a schedule for honey production. I can't simply disassemble a hive, break up the colony and sell a new, prospective beekeeper some bees without incurring an interruption in my honey production. Selling bees means I have to charge enough to replace the honey that won't be produced.

The best time to acquire bees is in the early spring, and there are beekeepers who do nothing but sell bees. They don't care about making honey. Their purpose (here I go again) for keeping bees is to sell honeybees to aspiring new beekeepers, or lazy beekeepers who don't take care of their bees and complain how there's no money in beekeeping.

As you order your bees in the late winter (you can find all kinds of advertisements in the magazines I begged you to subscribe to), you will order them for delivery in the early spring. In the early spring, the queen will lay eggs and the colony will build up a population of foragers who will gather nectar and later turn it into honey. By the time spring starts turning into summer, the hive ought to be in full production. This is when most people who want bees are thinking about getting started.

Wrong.

You want to start thinking about getting started in the winter when it's cold and no one is thinking about raising bees. Order your equipment in the winter. Put it together in the winter. Order your bees, in the winter, to arrive in the early spring and put them to work. On this schedule, the colony will be ready to gather nectar and make honey, hopefully, enough honey to support themselves and a little extra for yourself.

Summer is too late to establish a hive, though in some cases it may work. And in the summer, the demand for bees is so high you won't likely find bees. It's like coming to the dance when the band is packing up and they're cleaning up the decorations.

Under normal circumstances, you'll order your bees in the winter and acquire them in the early spring. Let the population build up, and when summer arrives and everything bursts into bloom, the colony has a sufficient workforce to gather nectar and make some honey.

Then in late summer, when the blooming plants begin to diminish, you can think about harvesting honey. In the late summer, the queen will also begin to slow down her egg laying production. By fall, the bees will quietly begin to hunker down for winter and eat the honey you left them. During winter, the queen will not lay any eggs. This seasonality is described in full detail in most of the books I asked you to read.

Then, when the Mother Nature awakens the Created Order the following year in the early spring, the queen starts laying eggs again, the population builds up, by summer they're packing the hive with nectar and making honey and by late summer you'll have a honey harvest.

Understanding this seasonality will guide your management decisions. If you understand why you are keeping bees, that is, what's your purpose, you need to understand the seasonal fluctuations. Even the older books from the library with the pretty librarian will have this information in it.

I'm almost always asked, "Do you harvest your honey all year?" The simple answer is, "no." The best analogy, again, is a garden. Do I harvest my sweet corn all year? Obviously the answer is, "no."

In the spring, I till the soil, spread fertilizer, then plant the seed. Do you know when I ordered the seed? In the dead of winter when no one was thinking about gardening! So I plant my seeds, spend eight to ten weeks pulling weeds and insuring the soil is moist enough to support the growth, and if there's no rain, I irrigate.

Then when the corn is ready, I pick some to eat fresh, give some to the neighbors, then I pick a bunch to freeze or can. Once in the freezer, I enjoy my corn all year long, but the harvest is but one or two really busy weeks in the late summer.

Beekeeping is like this. I spend all spring building up my population of honey bees. They spend all summer gathering nectar and turning it into honey. Then in the late summer, I spend one or two really busy weeks harvesting my honey.

The volume of honey I harvest is obviously more than I can immediately eat or sell, so I store my honey in five-gallon plastic, food-grade buckets. Then, when I go to sell my honey at the farmers market, I pour honey from the five-gallon bucket into the jars or squeeze bears I think my customers want.

And how I manage my bees is dependent upon my purpose...just like my purpose in raising sweet corn in the garden. I could be more commercial and expand my garden to plant more sweet corn, pick it and sell it at the farmers market. But my purpose in growing sweet corn is to fill my freezer and give away some corn to my neighbors.

Could I make money selling sweet corn? Sure! But that's not my purpose and so my gardening activities are guided and limited to suit my purpose. So it is with honey bees and bee keeping.

Everything has a seasonality about it. Beekeeping is no exception. If you wait until summer to get your bees, about the only thing they'll do is build up a population for winter and maybe gather enough honey to get them through the winter.

Maybe.

If the fall weather cuts the bloom short or if you are in a drought, you may have to feed sugar syrup to insure they will survive the winter. Feeding sugar is an extra expense.

Beekeeping, like gardening, is so dependent upon the weather. But your ability and management skill also counts.

Nucs:

Okay, so where do you get your bees? The logical source is from a beekeeper. As I mentioned in the last chapter, some beekeepers do nothing but sell bees. That's their purpose. If you ask around in your bee club, someone will help you find bees, and some bee clubs will band together and order a bunch of bees (packages or nucs) at discounted prices.

Now some beekeepers will sell you a small hive in the early spring. It may be a single story, fully-functional hive, ready to go.

Or a beekeeper may sell you what is called a "nuc," an abbreviated word for "nucleus." A nuc is nothing but a starter hive, or a miniature version of a hive comprised of four or five frames of bees, brood and some honey and pollen.

Nucs are sold by beekeepers who buy or raise early-season queens and divide their over-wintered colonies, leaving the old queen with the original hive and implanting the early-season queen into the split. Some beekeepers specialize in making early-season nucs. It's their purpose and it's how they make their income.

If I were starting off in beekeeping, I would find a supplier of nucs, or if I knew a beekeeper, I would ask him or her to order some queens and make me some splits. To do this, you need to have your equipment ready as the beekeeper may want to put the new queen and the split hive into your hive body. This is why you start your beekeeping in the winter. You need to be prepared and have your equipment ready.

Further, some beekeepers specialize in nuc production, but if you know of a beekeeper, they may be kind enough to make you a few splits. Splits are nucs. There I go again with the jargon. If you want a nuc, you'll find a beekeeper at your local bee meeting who can fix you up. But you have to place your order early. Many nucs and splits are sold out by the time the new beekeeper wants to buy.

I get calls asking if I sell bees, usually in the early summer when my bees are working. I politely tell them I don't. I've made nucs, both for my expansion and for sale, and nuc production is a specialized part of beekeeping. It's done in the early spring. It's not something I have time to pursue once my bees start their production of honey.

But if you are interested in starting in beekeeping, it is my opinion that a nuc is the best way to go. Check with your local bee club as some local beekeepers sell nucs and splits, or would be willing to make some for you. Or grab your trusty bee magazine and search the classified magazines for nuc suppliers.

Almost exclusively, nucs must be picked up, in person. Due to increasingly complex shipping regulations, nucs are no longer shipped.

If you come to this party a little late, and you cannot find local nucs or no one will make you a split, do not despair, packages are a perfectly suitable option...and you can order a package through the mail!

Packages:

The second option is to buy a package. Again, search out the ads in your bee magazines as package suppliers all advertise. With a nuc, you'll have to physically drive to the beekeeper's place and pick it up. Packages can be mailed to you. But check with your supplier and ask at your local post office. The authorities are cracking down on shipping anything living because these critters often die in transit.

Now here's one drawback about packages of bees and shipping costs. The shipping charges have escalated every year and it's more expensive than it used to be. If you buy one package, the last time I checked, the shipping charges were $22. Now if you buy two packages, the total shipping charges jump to $31, which isn't too bad per package as they bundle these two packages together. When you buy three packages, the shipping comes to $38 and four packages (the most they can bundle together) was $41.

Obviously, it pays to order more than one package.

Additionally, rules and regulations change every year and the post office is becoming more reluctant to ship "live" animals. Our local post office handles boxes of day-old baby chicks, as well as bees, and it's getting harder and harder to guarantee live delivery. Some post offices absolutely hate bees and will abuse the shipment like leaving the crate out on cold loading docks.

I have nothing but praise for my local post office, but then I go in a week before I expect the bees to arrive and alert them of my pending arrival. When the bees come in, they call me so I can come right down and pick them up in the early morning. I don't want my bees riding around town in a hot vehicle. I offer to pick them up from the loading dock first thing in the morning, usually around six o'clock. I also request my shipper call me when the order is shipped.

Now a package is nothing more than 3,000 bees shaken into a wire cage. They have a new, unfamiliar queen introduced to them. Your job is to take this package home, set the queen (restrained in her own cage) into the hive, then dump the wire cage of bees into the hive. In a few days, the queen will emerge from her cage. Hopefully, by this time the bunch of bees have become familiar with her special queen scent and won't kill her. She will be released and can start laying eggs. After twenty-one days, the first new generation of bees emerges.

Packages of bees offer a slow start to establishing a colony of bees. While waiting those twenty-one days, some of the bees that came with the package begin to die of old age. Some bees will die the first day you put them in the hive. Then, after twenty-one days, more bees emerge and the population begins to swing upward.

A nuc, on the other hand, is a split from the original colony that contains four or five frames of bees, larvae, sealed pupae and emerging adult bees. Your new generation of bees will come out the first day the nuc is established. Nucs are like taking a running start at beekeeping, while a package is like getting out of bed and trying to find your shoes.

Both will work, but nucs are greatly preferred, in my opinion. Oddly, and depending on your source of nucs or packages, your cost will be about the same. Some of you will not have a local beekeeper so you will have to pay the shipping charges on top of the price of the package.

You can expect to pay somewhere in the neighborhood of $75 to $100 per package plus shipping. Nucs will run $100 to $125 and the cost of shipping (the convenience of delivery) makes the package as costly as a nuc.

But the nuc will out-perform your package every time. And yet, with all the advantages I see in buying an up-and-running nuc, the vast majority of new beekeepers prefer the slumbering packages. I'm not sure I understand why.

<u>Swarms</u>:

There is another way to get bees but it is far less reliable. But it is free!

You can put your name in with the local police and fire station to pick up and retrieve swarms. Now bear in mind, as I've been keeping bees in this area for over 20 years, I've got my name on these lists and have enough name recognition that I get ample calls. You have to work your way into this system.

Further, when the call comes, you have to go. Swarms don't wait for you and sometimes they're forty feet in the air. Most new beekeepers work and you don't have the flexibility or the equipment to take off and go.

And you cannot schedule a swarm for the early spring. Some swarms come so late they never really build up for the winter and you'll have to feed them.

But swarms are free. But you also need to know something about bees to understand how to capture a swarm. Some years are more "swarmy," that is more swarms are reported. Some years the level of swarming is surprising low. Swarms are free, but they are an unreliable source of bees...and you have to have equipment ready for them.

As you get more experience, you can set up "bait hives" that will attract and trap swarms. But that's another topic for another day. Check out my web site at www.smashwords.com for two resources on capturing swarms.

Specifically, type these two urls into your browser:

https://www.smashwords.com/books/view/133000
https://www.smashwords.com/books/view/133149

If you are seriously planning to start beekeeping, you will want to acquire your bees as early in the spring as possible. That means you need to have your bees ordered, or you've made arrangements with a local beekeeper in the early winter to purchase a nuc when the weather settles.

Some beekeepers may sell you a hive of bees as the summer commences, but most won't. Those bees are working. Or they may charge you a high price that also includes the anticipated honey that would have been harvested.

Location:

Okay, let's assume you've got your equipment ordered and you've made arrangements to acquire some bees. Now, where are you going to put them?

When that question is asked, many people assume they can put a hive of bees in the corner of the back yard, up against the solid privacy fence. This may work if a) you have a really big yard, b) you can keep the hive hidden from your neighbors, c) you can set it apart to keep your children out of it, and d) your city doesn't have an ordinance against bees, provided you live within city limits.

This also works if you have bees that are gentle and not aggressive, and there are no guarantees that your bees will have a sweet disposition for your back yard.

And remember how I thought it was best to start with four, and at minimum, two hives? Most neighbors may tolerate a single, small bee hive, especially if you share some of the honey you produce.

And in the first year, as the bees work to establish the colony and draw out the comb, the colony will likely remain fairly small. However, you won't have any honey produced that first year under normal circumstances.

But the second year, the over-wintered colony will start taking off. The population will begin to expand. You're going to need more boxes for incoming nectar. Adding more boxes, stacked higher and higher, will make that hive look pretty intimidating to the neighbors. If you don't add more boxes, the colony will grow and become crowded. Crowded conditions within the hive is the precursor for swarming.

A swarm is the naturally occurring event that happens when an over-wintered hive grows and expands. Once a certain level is reached, or if the colony feels crowded, the old queen leaves with half of the work force. The other half remains back home and the colony raises a new queen. This is an act of reproduction to insure the survival of the species.

That old queen and half the work force that leaves will fly out, usually within ten to fifty yards of the home hive. That translates to your neighbor's back yard. When the swarm comes out of the hive, the air is literally buzzing with bees. To those who don't know anything about bees, it is the cross between a horror movie and a plague of biblical proportions.

Once this flying, swirling mass of bees consolidates and clusters in your neighbor's yard, your neighbors will want to lock all the doors and windows and they'll call the police. The police then call me and I come and retrieve the swarm.

Or they may call you to get rid of your bees, or they may call their lawyer to see what can be done to shut you down.

When I retrieve a swarm, the typical question from the homeowner is, "Where did those bees come from?" I try and tell them that bees exist in hollow trees all over the neighborhood.

That's little comfort. They just want the bees gone, and if they find out you have bees and this is your swarm from your hives…well it won't be pretty.

And if the neighbor's eight-year old boy wanders over to that box of bees, <u>I will bet you a dollar</u> he's going to get stung.

Never mind the hive is on your property. Never mind you had a fence to keep him out. Never mind he should know better or his parents should be keep better track of their children. Bee hives attract eight-year old boys like a magnet. And eight-year old little boys just have to probe the entrance with a stick. It's in our D.N.A. And the bees will come out and sting this two-legged intruder. It's going to get ugly real fast.

And you owe me a dollar because this bet is a sure thing! After all, I was once an eight-year old boy! I understand what drives this madness.

The best place for bees is in a protected area like a wooded fence-row, on a farm, away from people and fenced off from livestock who may bump up against the hive or decide to scratch their hide on that nice corner.

The ideal place will have ample fields of forage, plenty of crops and blooms, wild flowers, ditch banks and access to water. If your bees, set in your back yard, need water, I will bet you another dollar they'll start looking for water in your neighbor's swimming pool, bird bath or pet bowl. And the neighbors won't like it. Even one dead, drowned bee in the pool filter will start an uproar.

Now you owe me two dollars.

Bees generally will leave anyone and anything alone. They have work to do. They don't bother you unless you bother them.

But the perceived danger is what will get you into trouble. The beginning beekeeping books will have a host of more tips on choosing a location, including what kind of hive stand to set the hive on. But it does amaze me. When I ask, "Where are you planning to put these bees?" the response comes, "Well, I was thinking in the back yard."

Before you get your bees, think through where you can place the hive. There are lots of farmers who would love to have some hives of bees on their farm. They usually want them in the corner of the field or in a fence row. Now, however, the issue becomes how you can have access to your hive on someone else's property and your ability to haul equipment from your garage to the farm.

And these are things beginning beekeepers just don't think about. And if you start keeping bees in your back yard, and the hive expands and becomes increasingly heavy, I can guarantee you it becomes harder to move. And as hives become bigger, the bees tend to less tolerant of intruders.

Be smart. Find a good location, away from the neighbors, so you don't have to move the bees. Don't presume a hive can be placed in the corner of the back yard. Bear in mind, some people do it, but the likelihood of a beginner doing it successfully is fairly small.

I have another resource at www.CreateSpace.com entitled, *Beekeeping 101: Where Can I Keep My Bees?* and you can also find it at my www.smashwords.com page at:

https://www.smashwords.com/books/view/51714

This resource goes into greater detail. Locating a hive is not a simple decision.

Mentors:

At a recent bee meeting, I met a woman who started some hives on her farm. She read where beginners are better off starting several hives instead of one, so she decided she would start off with eight.

Now eight hives for a beginner is not out of the question, so she got hold of some catalogs and ordered the equipment. She then ordered eight packages of bees. And she felt she needed some extracting equipment so she found brand new extracting equipment in the catalog.

She told me that she spent $6,000 (yes, six *thousand* dollars) on those eight hives, packages and extracting equipment.

Ouch! That seemed way too high. But whatever she ordered had to be shipped.

Add another, "ouch!"

All those wooden boxes were heavy and had to be shipped by truck freight. She didn't have a loading dock so they had to be unloaded at the warehouse and shipped by private carrier.

Double "ouch!"

The she said she didn't get any honey that first year.

Ouch!

She was asking me why she didn't get any honey that first year. She thought for sure she should have gotten some. Her consistent statement was, "Six thousand dollars and not a drop of honey to show for it."

Well, I tried to point out that starting her beekeeping enterprise with packages didn't help her cause, and the first year the bees had to draw out all that wax foundation into honey comb. So not getting honey that first year was not totally out of the question. I suggested she should have gone with nucs.

Her response was, "But we didn't have anyone to mentor us." (Yeah, let's blame someone else...it's not your fault, is it?).

What she meant was, she didn't have anyone around who sold nucs (meaning another beekeeper) nor did she have someone who could have told her that packages would not likely produce any honey that first year.

Ouch!

Apparently everything she did she read in a book. And that's not all bad. I applaud her fortitude of jumping into a venture with a lot of courage and faith. But a mentor might have guided her differently, or shared with her what works in her area.

As more and more people call me about getting started in bees, I have to wonder how serious they are about this project. There have been some people who ordered equipment and bees, then asked if I could mentor them.

That term, "mentor," is used very generally and loosely. I didn't exactly look over their shoulder, but I did make a few phone calls to see what was going on (and most of them didn't quite have the nerve to open their hives).

I also made a couple of on-farm visits and we opened the hive together. If you're going to start keeping bees, you have to have enough fortitude to do the work. I'm limited in the number of on-farm visits I can make and the number of new beekeepers I can mentor.

I keep trying to convey to people that my time is limited. And no one really wants to pay me for my time for what it's worth to me. So, out of the goodness of my heart, I make these visits for free. Generally, I choose two beginning beekeepers to mentor each year and that's about my limit.

The idea of a mentor is one who will look over your shoulder, assist with questions, and basically be a guide along the seasonal path. Mentors should be great encouragers, and if nothing else, be there to hold your hand and tell you you're not crazy for wanting to raise bees. You're looking for a coach. Coaches give advice and encouragement, but coaches don't play the game. You do.

A mentor may also be a source of used equipment and nucs. Or they will have a couple of catalogs handy for you to borrow. I've given some equipment to some people wanting to start bees. I've asked for a couple of bucks or they promised me a gallon of honey when they harvest their first crop of honey.

In the end, it's become easier to simply give them a catalog or give them the website of my local supplier. I continue to pass my inquirers on to www.isabees.com, a delightful company run by two delightful people whom I highly respect. Jane and Scott are passionate about keeping bees. They are compassionate teachers and patient enablers for beginners. They do a much better job than me and I think they're the best in the business.

Concluding Thoughts:

As I keep bees, I continue to evaluate what I'm doing and what I can do differently and more efficiently. But I find I'm slowing down in my old age. I can't multi-task like I did in my younger days. I can't lift as many boxes for as long as I use to when I was young. Old age can be very discouraging. But I'm not giving up!

Would I do it all over again? Absolutely! Would I change a few things? Yeah!

I would have skipped all the used equipment I bought. I'd be better off making the investment with new equipment. Every year, the attrition of old bee boxes in my operation is staggering. And I hate throwing anything away. But for what I paid for them, I got my money's worth. Yet replacing the old equipment just takes more time and energy.

If you're really interested in keeping bees, I highly recommend joining a bee club. In my beginning days, there were no bee clubs in my area. I learned by flying by the seat of my pants and what I could read at the library. There was no Internet back then. Today, beekeeping is very popular. Beekeeping clubs are popping up all over and the Internet has helped us communicate on a global level.

When I moved to Missouri, I traveled an hour and fifteen minutes (one way) to attend a monthly bee keeping club. When that got to be too much, I started my own local club. I started by inviting the other three local beekeepers to get together on a Tuesday evening to talk about what's going on in our hives and what we could do for one another. Then some people who wanted to keep bees started showing up. They had questions. We had opinions. Then I decided I would teach a beekeeping course.

Our club has grown to probably fifty members and on that fourth Tuesday of the month, we may have twenty to twenty-five people show up. We have no officers, no by-laws, no money, no dues, no fees. We just show up and talk bees.

You could start your own club as well. Just find another beekeeper and meet together. Or go over to the other beekeeper's house and open their hive. Mentoring doesn't have to start with some white-haired, bearded old man who dispenses sage advice. Mentor each other. Mentoring ought to be mutual.

I'm also President of the Missouri State Beekeepers. I encourage people to start a local club and join the state organization. We have resources and run educational meetings to bring in expensive speakers who have national notoriety. State meetings provide tremendous networking opportunities. Many of the suppliers bring orders to these meetings saving the customer shipping charges.

One of the things I like about beekeeping is getting out to my bee yards and enjoying the solitude with the 600,000 bees living in those twenty hives. But I also enjoy teaching and sharing my knowledge.

I enjoy selling honey and making money. For me, beekeeping is a commercial enterprise, driven by profits which I can reinvest into my operation and provide a few luxuries for my family.

And I'm still learning. You never quit learning. You never reach that stage when you know it all.

When I went to college, my father drove me down to Iowa State University with some books and clothes. We checked into the dorm, unpacked the boxes, then went for a bite to eat (my father was famous for enjoying a slice of pie, preferably cherry or peach, with an afternoon cup of coffee).

As we ate, he shared many of his college memories. When he dropped me off at the dorm, he gave me wise words that have never left me. He said, "Enjoy college. It is the adventure of a lifetime."

Beekeeping is the same way. It is definitely an adventure, and if you stay in beekeeping long enough, it can be a very rewarding adventure.

Yet it grieves my heart to see so many casualties of well-intentioned people who have no clue of what they are getting into. They have no one to guide them as they get started. They have no one to hold their hand and say, "Yeah, it still hurts when I get stung, too." They give up too early and give away their equipment for too little money.

Beekeeping is a highly rewarding adventure. But there are advantageous ways to getting started, and ways that do nothing but challenge you from the starting gate. I hope you find a way that makes your beekeeping adventure most rewarding. I know it's been that way for me.

About the author:

Grant F.C. Gillard is a Presbyterian Pastor in Jackson, Missouri, husband and father. He is a part-time, commercial beekeeper keeping around 200 hives, give or take a handful depending on the time of year and how many swarms he has caught.

His methodology is best described as keeping bees as naturally as possible with sustainable practices including raising his own locally adapted queen honey bees.

He markets his honey through farmers markets, wholesale to grocery stores, and from his driveway with a self-service "honor box."

At the writing of this manuscript, Grant is the President of the Missouri State Beekeepers Association, whose web address is: http://www.mostatebeekeepers.org

Grant is a frequent conference speaker and has published numerous articles in both Bee Culture and American Bee Journal. Contact him for his availability for your next meeting at gillard5@charter.net

His other publications can be found on the web. For a complete listing of all his books, check out his web site at

www.grantgillard.weebly.com

Some of his fiction and short stories can be found on the web as well at https://www.smashwords.com/profile/view/beekeeper731

He blogs on www.xomba.com and www.expertscolumn.com

You can always find him on Facebook and Pinterest.

And if all else fails, "Google" him.

www.ingramcontent.com/pod-product-compliance
Lightning Source LLC
Chambersburg PA
CBHW072312290526
45794CB00002B/632